KNOWING GOD'S WILL

MADE EASY

Knowing God's Will Made Easy

Rose Publishing, LLC
P. O. Box 3473
Peabody, Massachusetts 01961-3473 USA
www.hendricksonrose.com

The *Made Easy* series is a collection of concise, pocket-sized books that summarize key biblical teachings and provide clear, user-friendly explanations to common questions about the Christian faith. Find more Made Easy books at www.hendricksonrose.com.

ISBN 9781628628234

Author: Len Woods

Printed in the United States of America
010220VP

CONTENTS

"For I have come down from heaven not to do my will but to do the will of him who sent me."

JESUS OF NAZARETH

John 6:38

This little book on knowing God's will is part of the *Made Easy* book series. If you've ever faced a life-changing decision, or ever looked up and asked that painful question, *Why Lord?*, then you know that God's will isn't always "easy." While understanding God's will might not be easy, it's certainly not impossible. God hasn't left us on our own to get lost. He has provided us with resources and guidance to show us a way out the fog, so that we can have a clear (or at least clear*er*) view of his will for our lives.

Few subjects generate more questions than "God's will."

- What do people mean when they say "the will of God"?
- Does the Bible suggest that God has a unique plan for our lives? If so, how detailed is that plan, and how can someone go about discovering it?
- Does God's sovereignty trump human freedom? (And, by the way, what does *sovereignty* even mean?)

- What happens when our plans and God's plans are not in sync?
- Is it possible for someone to completely miss God's will for their life?

We'll tackle questions like these (and others) in the following pages.

For readers who want to ponder the mystery of God's will further, or for those who want to go through this book with others, we've included some reflection and group discussion questions at the end.

GOD'S WILL: AN INTRODUCTION

Dorothy Gale wanted to go home to Kansas.

Rocky Balboa wanted to "go the distance."

Frodo the Hobbit wanted to destroy his magical ring before it destroyed him and those he loved.

We could keep going, but you get the point: Every memorable story features a character who wants something—and is willing to go to extraordinary lengths to get it.

This universal, unwritten rule also applies to the Bible. Though many regard God's Word as a religious rulebook or a quaint collection of ancient wisdom, it's actually a story. It's the *real-life* story of what happened when God, in sheer goodness and love, designed a perfect world with humans at the center.

Why would the Almighty do such a thing? Because—as the main character in the biggest and best story of all—he wanted something: creatures who would reflect his glory, live in his perfect love, and revel in his exquisite blessings.

If you're at all familiar with the Bible, you know that right at the start everything takes a disastrous turn. The human creatures defy their Creator. By their inexplicable rebellion, they plunge themselves and the world into ruin. Thankfully, the story isn't over. In fact, far from it. On the heels of this shocking plot twist, we get to glimpse the Almighty's overwhelming desire to rescue and recover all that he's lost. The rest of the Old and New Testaments demonstrate the stunning lengths to which God is willing to go to get what he wants.

This, in essence, is the story of the Bible, the story of the universe, the story of us. From Genesis to Revelation, we read about what God has done (and is doing still) to win back the hearts of rebels, to eradicate evil, and to make all things new.

Turns out that we can't really know the *will* of God apart from the *story* of God.

WHAT DOES "GOD'S WILL" MEAN?

The Greek noun *thelema,* often translated as *will* in the Bible, is related to a verb that means, "to want, desire, or like." When the Bible speaks about God's will, it's referring to the things the Almighty *wants* to see happen, the things he *desires* to do for his people, and the acts he'd *like* for his people to engage in (or not). Those are the outcomes that fill him—and us—with deep joy.

"God's will" or "the will of God" refer to the plans and purposes of God that spring from his perfect desires. Much of his will has already been revealed the Bible. Some of God's will remains a mystery for at least two reasons: because Scripture doesn't tell us everything and because history is still unfolding.

When Christians say to one another, "Pray that I'll know God's will," typically they're referring to a specific life situation in which they have more than one option. For example, they're . . .

- Pondering school choices.

  Should I go to that out-of-state college or stick with my local school? Would it be wise, or nuts, for me to go back to school at my age?

- Weighing employment possibilities.

  Should I take the job offer in Amarillo . . . or start looking in Topeka . . . or just keep the job I have?

- Mulling over a big purchase.

  Should I put an offer on the older but larger house or the newer one?

- Wondering about a romantic relationship.

  Is this "the one" or does God want me to keep looking?

As we will see, God's will certainly involves locations and vocations, money and matrimony, but it's much more expansive than that.

VIEWS ON GOD'S WILL

When it comes to thinking about God and what his will for us means, people tend to fall at many different points along a spectrum, depending on how they view God. (The following is somewhat exaggerated to make that point.)

The Micromanager

On one end of the spectrum, God is viewed as the great Micromanager of the universe. He is the ultimate, infinite, controlling "Helicopter Parent," meaning he has got his hands in *every* detail. The "will of God" is a kind of divine blueprint, a highly detailed itinerary for the most satisfying life possible. From this perspective, it's easy to imagine God discussing with Gabriel, Michael, and the other angels his detailed, ideal plan for each person's life:

> "And so I'm going to arrange for little Joey, at age nine, to come down with a serious case of poison oak. This isn't to punish him; it's to get him to see that my plan for him is to become a dermatologist. This means, of course, I want him making straight A's in high school so that he can get into Yale for his undergrad studies and then go to Harvard for

> med school. Later, while he's doing his fellowship in New York City, my will is for him to meet Lindsay, his perfect soul mate (talk about a match made in heaven!). And after that . . . "

Maybe you tend to view God like this. You sincerely try to follow God's guidance moment by moment, so that you can—hopefully—stay right in the center of his will. You pray about *every* decision and look for confirmation in all choices. You think that this is the only way to be in exactly the right place at precisely the right time—to meet "Mr./Ms. Right," to land the perfect job, and so forth. This understanding of the will of God pictures life rather like a complex maze with only one ideal solution. Take a wrong turn and you'll miss out on untold blessings. Navigate with perfect obedience, and you'll win the jackpot of joy!

But what if, in a moment of uncertainty or a season of bullheadedness, a person takes a wrong turn? Suppose, for example, at the age of nine, when little Joey comes down with that divinely ordained case of poison oak, he starts playing video games to take his mind off his incessant itching. And what if while doing that he thinks, *I want to design video games when I grow up!* And suppose he never even considers an Ivy League education and heads west to a job in California where he never even meets Lindsay from NYC? Does that mean that from the age of nine onward, Joe has completely missed God's will?

For many believers this view of God's will has a paralyzing effect. It can leave us walking around with a nervous, sick feeling that we could be just one careless decision away from ruining our life. String together enough bad choices and before we even reach the age of 30, we could very easily be on God's 4,157th best plan! Talk about a depressing prospect!

The AWOL God

Another view of God's will imagines a God who made the world and then went, well . . . God only knows where! This is the AWOL God, the ultimate "free range" parent. Expect this deity (if you ever can find him) to be impersonal, disinterested, and uninvolved in the day-to-day affairs of the world. (And don't think for a moment he's losing sleep about where you work or live, or whom you might marry!)

To some, this view of God's will is exhilarating. You get to create whatever life you choose and don't have to worry about what God might want you to do. To others, this idea is overwhelming and distressing—like trying to go from California to Hawaii . . . in a canoe . . . without a compass.

The Captain

There are many ways to think about God's will in between these two extremes. A quick survey of the Bible and all of Christian history shows the Almighty offering plenty of guidance and help, but also giving his human creatures all sorts of freedom and responsibility. God doesn't program and micromanage us, nor does he abandon us to figure out life on our own. Instead, God is very proactive:

- He gives us unique abilities, interests, passions, and creativity.
- He puts each of us in a part of the world filled with big opportunities and enormous needs.

- He provides some broad ground rules for life, chief among them being to love God and love others (Matthew 22:37–39).
- He encourages us. In effect, he says, "Within my gracious boundaries, go! Be bold! Attempt big things! Live your one unique life to the fullest. Walk with me and I'll be there for you every step of the way."

> "God will meet you where you are in order to take you where He wants you to go."
>
> TONY EVANS

God's not a divine micromanager with only one perfect, yet cryptic, will for each person's life. Nor is he an AWOL deity who says, "Do pretty much whatever. I don't care." Instead, God can be seen as (to use another imperfect metaphor) the omni-competent captain of the giant ocean liner called *life*. Because the ship is in the strong hands of an attentive, wise, good captain, we can relax. He is going to get us exactly where we're supposed to be.

WHAT ARE SOME WRONG ASSUMPTIONS ABOUT GOD'S WILL?

WRONG ASSUMPTION #1:
God's will is pretty much impossible for the average Christian to figure out.

Under this assumption, God's will is accessible only to a few, like eccentric Bible scholars or spiritual mystics who somehow have figured out how to hack into the Lord's heavenly database. God is pictured as a tough-as-nails professor who relishes the thought of flunking all those clueless believers enrolled in "God's Will 101." If we buy into this, we can start thinking, *This course is impossible to pass, much less ace! I should just go ahead and drop out and resign myself to being a mediocre believer who bumbles through life.*

Sorry, but that's wrong! False! Not true! God is not trying to turn the spiritual life into a big puzzle or a frustrating search. He wants us to know his will so that we can do it.

In the New Testament, the apostle Paul wrote about the importance of letting the truth of God shape our minds and lives so that we "will be able to test and approve what God's will is—his good, pleasing and perfect will" (Romans 12:2). In other words, God wants us to discern his purposes. Notice how Paul exhorts the Ephesian believers to strive to know God's will: "Therefore do not be foolish, but understand what the Lord's will is" (Ephesians 5:17). He prayed for the Colossian believers to know God's will: "For this reason, since the day we heard about you, we have not stopped praying for you. We continually ask God to fill you with the knowledge of his will through all the wisdom and understanding that the Spirit gives" (Colossians 1:9).

> "God plays no game of hide-and-seek—the closer you draw to the heart of God, the more clearly you'll know the will of God. He reveals His will day by day. He unrolls the scroll one line at a time."
>
> JUNE HUNT

If God meant for his will to be an unknowable mystery, the Spirit of God would never move Paul to pray such prayers or issue such challenges. The fact is God wants us to know his plan for our lives. He may not reveal details for tomorrow, next month, or next year, but he will give us whatever we need for this next moment.

WRONG ASSUMPTION #2:
If something is really fun and enjoyable, it must not be God's will.

Sometimes we can view God as a Cosmic Party Pooper, believing that he wants his people to be hyper-serious, even somber. We can take a grim-faced view of the Christian life and conclude, *Believers who are always smiling and enjoying life must be doing something wrong. There's no way God is pleased with that!* Before long, just hearing the phrase "the will of God" makes us wince. This is because we've made it synonymous with unwanted or bad things. We may find ourselves thinking thoughts like, *I'm not so sure I really want to seek God's will. After all, I might find it, and it'll surely involve all sorts of unpleasantness.* No wonder many young people, when considering a life spent doing the will of

God, wrestle with thoughts like this: *I just know that if I say to God, "not my will but yours be done," he'll reply, "Aha, gotcha!" Then he'll send me some place overseas where I'll hate living. I'll end up poor and single. And if God does ever allow me to get married, it'll be to someone who's boring or mean, and I'll be so miserable.*

If you sometimes struggle with such thoughts, maybe this is a good time to reread the following Bible verses:

***"For the LORD God is a sun and shield;
the LORD bestows favor and honor;
no good thing does he withhold from
those whose walk is blameless."***

PSALM 84:11

***"Give thanks to the LORD, for he is good;
his love endures forever."***

PSALM 107:1

"'For I know the plans I have for you,' declares the LORD, 'plans to prosper you and not to harm you, plans to give you hope and a future.'"

JEREMIAH 29:11

"He who did not spare his own Son,
but gave him up for us all—
how will he not also, along with him,
graciously give us all things?"
ROMANS 8:32

"The thief comes only to steal and kill and destroy; I have come that they may have life, and have it to the full."
JOHN 10:10

Someone once pointed out that if we really believed our heavenly Father is one-hundred percent good all the time, we'd trust that his will is always good. And if we trusted that, we would *do* his will as Jesus did (Matthew 26:42).

Let's say it again:

The Bible declares that God is good.

"Give thanks to the Lord, for he is good; his love endures forever" (Psalm 106:1).

He loves to give good gifts to his children.

"If you, then, though you are evil, know how to give good gifts to your children, how much more will your Father in heaven give good gifts to those who ask him!" (Matthew 7:11).

"Whence comes this idea that if what we are doing is fun, it can't be God's will? The God who made giraffes, a baby's fingernails, a puppy's tail, a crooknecked squash, the bobwhite's call, and a young girl's giggle, has a sense of humor. Make no mistake about that."

CATHERINE MARSHALL

He wants his followers to have the richest life imaginable.

"The thief comes only to steal and kill and destroy; I have come that they may have life, and have it to the full" (John 10:10).

He desires that we be full of joy.

"I have told you this so that my joy may be in you and that your joy may be complete" (John 15:11).

It's by following Christ wholeheartedly that we find God's will: a life that honors God, blesses others, and brings happiness to our own souls.

WRONG ASSUMPTION #3:
If something is really hard and painful, it must not be God's will.

The flaw in this thinking is the notion that God *only* wants his people doing pleasant, fun, easy, comfortable things.

Nothing in the Bible suggests this is true.

Take the Old Testament prophets, for example. Nobody ever had a tougher job description: to deliver blunt, unpopular truth to hard-hearted souls. God actually told the prophet Jeremiah upfront, "They will not listen to you" (Jeremiah 7:27). Sure enough, as Jeremiah and the other prophets faithfully carried out the will of God for their lives, they were dismissed, mocked, beaten, and sometimes martyred.

> **"Emotional peace and calm . . . come after doing God's will and not before."**
>
> **ERWIN LUTZER**

Consider Jesus. Remember his baptism? Remember how God spoke audibly from heaven, expressing how much he loved Jesus and how pleased he was with him (Matthew 3:17)? Keep reading. The very next verse says the Spirit of God promptly led Jesus into the wilderness to face one of the hardest experiences of his life (Matthew 4:1)!

The Bible makes it clear that servants of God who carry out the will of God—even perfectly—are not exempted from pain. The ultimate example is Jesus sweating drops of blood in the garden of Gethsemane and crying out, "Yet not my will, but yours be done" (Luke 22:42), just before being led to his execution.

Sometimes the very thing that God wants his people doing *is* the hard and painful thing. We can't assume that just because we're in a rough patch, we're outside the will of God.

WRONG ASSUMPTION #4:
If I'm not sure of God's will, I should just wait around and do nothing.

The Bible references plenty of occasions in which God directed his servants through dramatic visions, dreams, and other supernatural promptings to go and do very specific things. But in many other instances, they didn't have a specific plan from above. What did they do then? They devised the best, wisest, most God-honoring plans they could come up with, and then got busy—always giving God veto authority over their plans. Notice the language Paul used (emphasis added):

> "The place where God calls you to is the place where your deep gladness and the world's deep hunger meet."
>
> FREDERICK BUECHNER

"But as he left, he promised, 'I will come back if it is God's will.' Then he set sail from Ephesus."

ACTS 18:21

"But I will come to you very soon, if the Lord is willing."

1 CORINTHIANS 4:19

". . . so that I may come to you with joy,
by God's will, and in your
company be refreshed."
ROMANS 15:32

James encouraged this same kind of active, trusting, open-handed approach for all believers:

"Now listen, you who say,
'Today or tomorrow we will go to this
or that city, spend a year there,
carry on business and make money.'
Why, you do not even know what will
happen tomorrow. What is your life?
You are a mist that appears
for a little while and then vanishes.
Instead, you ought to say,
'If it is the Lord's will,
we will live and do this or that.'"
JAMES 4:13–15

Rather than a lifestyle of passive waiting, it seems a lifestyle of active humility is commended in Scripture.

BUT WHAT ABOUT WHEN YOU'RE STUCK, FROZEN AT A CROSSROADS?

"You can't steer a parked car."

This sounds like the sort of statement a grandparent or a wise old counselor would make. And guess what? It's true. When you're unclear about which option is best—in spite of praying and weighing out the pros and cons and consulting wiser souls—you ultimately have to make a choice and get moving. You can't sit around waiting for heaven to drop a detailed forty-year plan in your lap. News flash: That's never going to happen!

Instead, take a deep breath and then a single step of faith. As you do, pray, "Lord, don't let me do something foolish here." Keep moving forward, prayerfully and carefully, asking the Lord all along the way to stop you—to tackle you if necessary—and redirect you if or when you start moving in an unwise direction. As you go, pray the prayer of the psalmist: "Teach me to do your will, for you are my God; may your good Spirit lead me on level ground" (Psalm 143:10).

THE FOUR *P*'S OF GOD'S WILL: PREDETERMINED, PREFERRED, PERMISSIVE, AND PERSONAL

A careful reading of the Bible seems to show different nuances in the phrase "God's will." Various passages in Scripture describe what we might label as God's predetermined will, his preferred will, his permissive will, and his personal will. Let's look briefly at each of those broad categories.

GOD'S PREDETERMINED WILL

Many passages of Scripture mention God sovereignly—and unilaterally—deciding (or foreordaining) certain things in eternity past. We see this in words, phrases, and verses like the following (emphasis added):

"For those God foreknew he also predestined to be conformed to the image of his Son."

ROMANS 8:29

"He chose us in him before the foundation of the world. In love he predestined us for adoption to sonship."

EPHESIANS 1:4–5

"In him we were also chosen, having been predestined according to the plan of him who works out everything in conformity with the purpose of his will."

EPHESIANS 1:11

"We are God's handiwork, created in Christ Jesus to do good works, which God prepared in advance for us to do."

EPHESIANS 2:10

"[Jesus was] handed over to you by God's deliberate plan and foreknowledge."

ACTS 2:23

"God's elect . . . have been chosen according to the foreknowledge of God the Father."

1 PETER 1:2

Theologians call this idea that things happen because God has predetermined that they will happen the "decree of God." This is God's predetermined will, sometimes called his sovereign will or prevailing will. Here, then, is that old familiar saying, "Everything happens for a reason"—with huge theological overtones.

Though all this is mysterious to ponder, it's crucial to remember that according to the Bible, God has an eternal plan to save sinful people, and nothing can alter or hinder this plan because it's rooted in God's all-powerful, unchanging character. Is there any way that something unforeseen might suddenly pop up and change the Almighty's plans? No! God does not speak without acting, nor promise without fulfilling (Numbers 23:19). He declares, "I the Lord do not change" (Malachi 3:6).

To summarize: Sovereignty means that nothing is random or accidental, that the universe is never out of control. The angels have never and will never hear God say "Whoops!" or "Uh-oh!" God is in and over, behind and underneath all the details of life.

WHAT DO WE MEAN BY "SOVEREIGNTY"?

When Christians say, "God is sovereign," what they mean is that God is the mighty King of everything. He is in charge. Despite how things may look or sometimes seem, God is ruling the universe and reigning over our lives. In short, nothing happens outside of his control. Here are some ways the Bible describes this idea:

"[God] made a decree for the rain
and a path for the thunderstorm."

JOB 28:26

"He does as he pleases with the powers
of heaven and the peoples of the earth.
No one can hold back his hand
or say to him: 'What have you done?'"

DANIEL 4:35

"The Lord foils the plans of the nations;
he thwarts the purposes of the peoples.
But the plans of the Lord stand firm
forever, the purposes of his heart
through all generations."

PSALM 33:10–11

*"The Lord does whatever pleases him,
in the heavens and on the earth,
in the seas and all their depths."*

PSALM 135:6

*"The Lord works out everything
to its proper end—even the wicked
for a day of disaster."*

PROVERBS 16:4

*"In their hearts humans plan their course,
but the Lord establishes their steps."*

PROVERBS 16:9

*"Many are the plans in a person's heart,
but it is the Lord's purpose that prevails."*

PROVERBS 19:21

*"Are not two sparrows sold for a penny?
Yet not one of them will fall to the ground
outside your Father's care."*

MATTHEW 10:29

Throughout history, the people of God have wrestled with questions about the ways God's sovereignty works out in daily life.

Can anything happen outside of God's sovereignty?

> No! If something could happen (come into being or come to pass) apart from God's sovereignty, then it would mean that the universe is subject to another power, cause, or deity that rivals the sovereign God revealed in the Bible. Yet the God of the Bible declares, "apart from me there is no God" (Isaiah 45:5). This means that anything and everything that happens must be, in some sense, the "will of God."

This conclusion naturally makes us uncomfortable, and so we ask a further question. How does God *will* these things?

> God wills some things directly, that is, necessarily. Gravity, for example, necessarily works according to the law God has decreed/established for it. If you have ever dropped a bowling ball on your foot, you understand this all too well.
>
> God wills other things indirectly; that is, they occur by means of creatures with the freedom to make choices.

From the point of view of God's omniscience (his knowledge of all things, including his foreknowledge of the future), these autonomous choices of creatures are certain to happen. But they are not *necessary* in the same way that the behavior of gravity is. God does not coerce choice. It is a great mystery, but in the plan of God, divine sovereignty and human responsibility are not at odds. They work seamlessly. Both are true.

But if we say that God is in complete control of the world—and the world is full of evil—doesn't this logically make God the author of evil?

The Bible is clear that the Lord is holy (Leviticus 20:26). In him is no darkness at all (1 John 1:5). He doesn't tempt anyone to do evil (James 1:13). In giving his created beings freedom to make choices, God permits evil and allows bad things to happen.

"But why?" we cry.

The answer to this question is complicated. We finite humans cannot completely comprehend the mind and purpose of an infinite God. But some things may be said about the existence of evil in an originally good creation. The possibility for evil must be present for created beings (like angels or humans) to be truly free and responsible beings. And that is what the Bible says. It is our choice to love and trust God or to reject him (Deuteronomy 30:19; John 5:40; 7:17). Think about it: If we were preprogrammed to obey God, we'd be nothing more than flesh-and-blood robots. Love that is forced isn't real love. The presence of evil maximizes the beauty of the gospel and the glory of God's plan, in the same way that a diamond sparkles more brilliantly against a dark velvet background. But let's be careful here. We are not saying that evil is a good thing. We are saying that God can redeem the ugly reality of evil in our lives and in the world, and that he will use it all to lead us to a better world.

GOD'S PREFERRED WILL

As mentioned earlier, the common Greek word for *will* (*thelema*) can mean "desire, pleasure, or wish." To speak of "God's will" refers to God's heart desire to see certain things come to pass. This is often described as his preferred will. This explains why we see verses instructing believers to live in ways that will please God (2 Corinthians 5:9; Ephesians 5:10; Colossians 1:10). It's why we see, in other places, clear references to things that the Lord does not want to see happen—like see wicked people die in their rebellion or see little ones perish (Matthew 18:14; 1 Timothy 2:3–4; 2 Peter 3:9).

> "There is only one way of victory over the bitterness and rage that comes naturally to us—to will what God wills brings peace."
>
> AMY CARMICHAEL

There are also all the things that God wants his people doing on a daily basis. Sometimes called God's prescriptive will, this consists of the commands for living that Jesus taught his disciples and told them to pass on to others (Matthew 28:18–20). This is the "apostle's teaching" to which the first Christians were devoted (Acts 2:42). At the most practical level, it's all that the Bible calls Christians to be and do. We find God's prescriptive will in the Holy Scriptures. Properly understood, the Bible gives us very clear guidelines and specific boundaries for how to live. (We'll talk more about this just ahead.)

"This is good, and pleases God our Savior, who wants all people to be saved and to come to a knowledge of the truth."
1 TIMOTHY 2:3–4

". . . so that you may live a life worthy of the Lord and please him in every way: bearing fruit in every good work, growing in the knowledge of God, being strengthened with all power according to his glorious might so that you may have great endurance and patience, and giving joyful thanks to the Father."
COLOSSIANS 1:10–12

DON'T REJECT GOD'S WILL

The Bible also speaks grimly and sadly of those who openly spurn God and rebel against his will.

"They rebelled against God's commands and despised the plans of the Most High."
PSALM 107:11

"'Woe to the obstinate children,' declares the Lord, 'to those who carry out plans that are not mine, forming an alliance, but not by my Spirit, heaping sin upon sin.'"
ISAIAH 30:1

"But the Pharisees and the experts in the law rejected God's purpose for themselves."
LUKE 7:30

"Jerusalem, Jerusalem, you who kill the prophets and stone those sent to you, how often I have longed to gather your children together, as a hen gathers her chicks under her wings, and you were not willing."

MATTHEW 23:37

Perhaps recalling those sobering words of Christ about the Pharisees and the people of Jerusalem, the apostle John said, "The world and its desires pass away, but whoever does the will of God lives forever" (1 John 2:17). The apostle Peter spoke of believers not living "the rest of their earthly lives for evil human desires, but rather for the will of God" (1 Peter 4:2).

GOD'S PERMISSIVE WILL

We could define God's permissive will as him sovereignly allowing difficult or even evil things to take place, but then subverting those things in surprising ways to bring about his predetermined will, which is his ultimate, eternal purposes.

Think, for example, of the biblical story of Joseph (see Genesis 37–50). God permitted Joseph's envious, older brothers to sell him to a caravan of Midianite traders who were headed to Egypt. God allowed these money-grubbing traders to sell Joseph as a slave to a high-ranking Egyptian government official. God watched as the wife of this official falsely accused Joseph of attempted rape. God then permitted Joseph to languish in prison for an extended period for a crime he didn't commit.

> "The basic purpose of prayer is not to bend God's will to mine, but to mold my will to His."
>
> TIMOTHY KELLER

In time, God ultimately pulled Joseph from the depths of prison and used all the evil choices by others and Joseph's painful circumstances to accomplish his divine plan. The Lord used Joseph to help many thousands of people survive a seven-year famine. When it was all over, the non-bitter

Joseph was reunited with his family and was able to say to his shocked brothers:

> *So then, it was not you who sent me here,*
> *but God. He made me father to Pharaoh,*
> *lord of his entire household*
> *and ruler of all Egypt. . . .*
> *You intended to harm me,*
> *but God intended it for good to*
> *accomplish what is now being done,*
> *the saving of many lives.*
>
> GENESIS 45:8; 50:20

Similarly—but of much greater significance—God permitted evil men to condemn and crucify his Son, Jesus (Acts 2:22–24). Yet in his wisdom and power, God willed the death of the innocent Christ to accomplish his eternal purpose of securing salvation for guilty sinners.

CAN DOING GOD'S WILL LEAD TO OR INVOLVE SUFFERING?

The short, not-so-popular, answer is *yes*.

From beginning to end, the Bible shows the people of God encountering trials and hardships. As they sought to live according to God's revealed will, neither Jewish believers nor later gentile Christians, neither Old Testament prophets nor New Testament apostles were exempted from suffering. In fact, Christ himself told his followers, "Everyone will hate you because of me" (Luke 21:17).

Peter experienced this reality firsthand. Called to be an apostle, he was persecuted simply for carrying out the Lord's will (Acts 5:18, 40–41; 12:1–5). Later, when writing to first century followers of Jesus who were suffering for their faith, Peter accepted persecution as a given, saying, "For it is better, if it is God's will, to suffer for doing good than for doing evil. . . . So then, those who suffer according to God's will should commit themselves to their faithful Creator and continue to do good" (1 Peter 3:17; 4:19).

This isn't a fun message to hear; however, believers don't have to despair. Jesus is our model and our hope. The Savior who insisted he came "to do the will of him who sent me" (John 6:38) and who added, "I always do what pleases him" (John 8:29) suffered horribly—but only briefly. After doing the will of God, he was "highly exalted" by God (Philippians 2:9; also Acts 2:33; 5:31). In God's perfect plan, it's glory, not suffering, that will have the last word.

"Therefore we do not lose heart.
Though outwardly we are wasting away,
yet inwardly we are being renewed
day by day.
For our light and momentary troubles
are achieving for us an eternal glory
that far outweighs them all.
So we fix our eyes not on what is seen,
but on what is unseen,
since what is seen is temporary,
but what is unseen is eternal."

2 CORINTHIANS 4:16–18

GOD'S PERSONAL WILL

God's personal will refers to God's very specific guidance of (or plan for) individuals. We see examples of this frequently in the book of Acts:

An angel of the Lord showed up and told Philip to go have a spiritual conversation with a confused Ethiopian official on a desert road.

Acts 8:26–39

Ananias had a vision in which the Lord told him to go meet the newly converted Saul.

Acts 9:10–19

Peter was directed by the Spirit in a vision to welcome Cornelius and his fellow gentiles into God's household.

Acts 10

The leaders of the church in Antioch were told by the Holy Spirit to set apart Saul and Barnabas for a special mission trip.

Acts 13:1–4

Paul and his missionary team were blocked (supernaturally) from venturing into Asia, but then summoned to Europe through the famous vision known as the Macedonian call.

Acts 16:6–10

Many believers read such biblical stories with wide eyes and say, *Angelic visits? Visions? The audible voice of God? I've never had any experiences like that!* Some reason, *I guess that means God no longer directs his people in personal and specific ways?* However, before you come to that conclusion, consider some "common" ways God might be revealing his personal will. Let's suppose these two scenarios:

A friend calls and invites Emma to a small group Bible study. She is resistant, even reluctant. But in the end she goes . . . and it's an awesome experience! For several months she undergoes spiritual growth like never before! So, do you think it might have been God's will for Emma's friend to invite her to the Bible study—and for Emma to go? Does God only reveal his personal will by spectacular means? Or can God's "good, pleasing, and perfect will" (Romans 12:2) present itself to us through something as ordinary as a phone call?

Next, let's suppose you're sitting mindlessly in bumper-to-bumper rush hour traffic, and the name and face of a dear friend flashes across your mind. You don't hear any heavenly voices, but you are struck by the thought, *I need to call*. You do, and as it turns out, the timing was perfect. Your friend was really low and in dire need of some encouragement. So, was all this coincidental? Or was God's Spirit behind it all, quietly revealing his desire for you in that moment through an unexpected nudge, a holy impression?

Obviously we have to be careful with these sorts of situations. Human experiences are subject to wildly divergent interpretations (John 12:29). What's more, Christians can (and do) claim all sorts of things, sometimes even ascribing mere human desires to God's will (like, *God told me you're supposed to go out with me!*).

To be sure, it's easy to misread an impulse, to make too much of flashing thoughts. Just because something seems like a *good* idea doesn't necessarily mean it's a *God* idea. But when an inclination isn't sinful or foolish or insensitive—and when it's rooted in love and genuine concern—why not? Who knows where it might lead, how God might use it . . . and us?

GOD'S WILL	WHAT IT MEANS	WHAT IT DOESN'T MEAN
Predetermined Will	God foreknows and sovereignly decrees all things. Nothing can hinder God's plans for his creation. Nothing catches him by surprise.	It doesn't mean that God causes humans to commit evil against their will.
Preferred Will	God desires good for our lives, including the way we should live, as summarized in the teaching of Jesus and the apostles.	It doesn't mean that humans, with the freedom to make choices, will always choose what is good.
Permissive Will	God allows evil circumstances and human choices that are not the good that he prescribes.	It doesn't mean that God makes people choose evil or that he considers evil a good thing.
Personal Will	God's specific and creative guidance of individual believers as they go about their lives.	It doesn't mean that God gives his people detailed, moment-by-moment instructions for every situation in life.

HOW DOES GOD REVEAL HIS WILL?

As we've said, God doesn't provide his children a detailed set of blueprints for life. Nobody gets a comprehensive itinerary for the next twenty, forty, or sixty years. Instead God gives believers his Word, his Spirit, his people, and his mission. With those resources, we are told to live by faith.

GOD'S WORD

As mentioned in the introduction, the Bible is not simply a rulebook, and it's surely not a divine day-planner. You can't flip it open and expect to find an explicit "to do" list for your day (with parenthetical, explanatory notes from the Almighty):

- Wear your khaki pants today. (I know it seems like an odd instruction, but trust me on this.)
- Go eat lunch at the new bistro—but avoid the house dressing! (I have somebody I want you to bump into there. Don't sit with your back to the door.)
- Start working on your resume. (Don't freak out. Breathe deeply . . . I've got this!)

On the contrary, the Bible is the wild but true story of God and his people. It's part *scrapbook*. It's verbal snapshots and stories, records and letters of what God is like, how he has acted in history and cared for his people. It's also part *guidebook.* It has examples of good and bad actions, sermons and commands, showing and telling modern-day readers the best and worst ways to live.

> "God's primary will for your life is not what job you ought to take . . . where you live or whether you get married or what house you ought to be in. God's primary will for your life is that you become a magnificent person in his image, somebody with the character of Jesus. . . . No circumstance can prevent that."
>
> JOHN ORTBERG

Since the Bible is God's *Word*, it shouldn't surprise us to find out it reveals God's *will*. Someone has suggested that about ninety percent of God's will for our lives is already spelled out in God's Word, and the rest is just details. That's about right. It doesn't matter if you're a teacher, a Fortune 500 CEO, or unemployed; if you live in New England, New Orleans, or New Zealand; if your dream is to adopt three children, or to open your own bakery, or to become an underwater welder, most of God's will is already spelled out for us. Here are just a handful of things that you can know—without a doubt—are God's will for you today if you are a follower of Jesus:

"Love the Lord your God with
all your heart and with all your soul
and with all your strength."
DEUTERONOMY 6:5; ALSO MARK 12:30

"A new command I give you:
Love one another. As I have loved you,
so you must love one another.
By this everyone will know that you are
my disciples, if you love one another."
JOHN 13:34–35

"Therefore do not be foolish,
but understand what the Lord's will is.
Do not get drunk on wine,
which leads to debauchery.
Instead be filled with the Spirit."
EPHESIANS 5:17–18

"Give thanks in all circumstances;
for this is God's will for you
in Christ Jesus."
1 THESSALONIANS 5:18

"For it is God's will that by doing good you should silence the ignorant talk of foolish people."
1 PETER 2:15

"Bear with each other and forgive one another if any of you has a grievance against someone. Forgive as the Lord forgave you."
COLOSSIANS 3:13

"It is God's will that you should be sanctified: that you should avoid sexual immorality."
1 THESSALONIANS 4:3

These, of course, are only a fraction of the clear-cut commands of Scripture. But as this handful of verses indicates, so much of God's will for our lives has zero to do with our geography, vocation, or marital status. It has to do with the kind of God-glorifying people he wants us to become.

You want a better handle on God's will for your individual life? Immerse yourself in God's inspired

Word. Declare the words of the psalmist: "I desire to do your will, my God; your law [instruction] is within my heart" (Psalm 40:8). According to Paul's final letter (2 Timothy 3:16–17), the holy Scriptures are profitable for teaching us (showing us what's right), reproving us (showing us where we're off track), correcting us (showing us how to get back on track), and training us in righteousness (showing us how to avoid straying in the future).

GOD'S SPIRIT

Knowing God's will isn't simply a matter of reading the Bible and then trying our hardest to do what it says. That approach is no different than the ancient people of God under the old covenant futilely trying to keep the Law of Moses. No, under the new covenant mediated by Christ (see Hebrews 8–10), God doesn't just tell us how to live from afar; he comes to live in and through us. New life in Christ isn't a matter of us having to rely on our own strength, it's us getting to rely on God's indwelling Spirit.

Consider all the Holy Spirit does to help believers know and do the will of our Father in heaven. The Spirit . . .

- Convicts people of sin. John 16:8
- Engineers spiritual life and growth. Titus 3:5
- Intercedes (prays for) the people of God. Romans 8:26–27
- Enables believers to serve God. Philippians 3:3
- Indwells believers. 1 Corinthians 6:19
- Leads believers in the way they should go. Romans 8:14
- Guides believers into truth and reveals "what is yet to come." John 16:13
- Strengthens the followers of Jesus to resist sinful urges. Galatians 5:17
- Makes it possible for believers to have access to God. Ephesians 2:18
- Gives believers supernatural abilities to use in building others up. 1 Corinthians 12:7–11
- Empowers Christians to share the good news of Jesus. Acts 1:8

- Prompts believers to carry out the specific will and purposes of God. Acts 13:4
- Produces godly character qualities in believers. Galatians 5:22–23; Philippians 1:6

What a resource! Not only do we have the treasure chest of truth that is the Word of God, we also have the Spirit of God to help us understand what God has said in his Word. It's as we humbly and diligently study the Scriptures that we find ourselves being taught, rebuked, corrected, equipped, and guided by the Spirit.

The New Testament also makes it clear that it is possible for believers to resist the work of the Spirit in our lives. We can "grieve the Holy Spirit of God" (Ephesians 4:30) or "quench the Spirit" (1 Thessalonians 5:19). Obviously, doing either is counter to doing the will of God.

Apart from the Spirit of truth guiding us in understanding and applying the word of truth, we really can't know God's will—much less do it.

The Spirit and the Word

Do you remember the promise Jesus made to his followers the night before he was crucified? Jesus said, "When he, the Spirit of truth, comes, he will guide you into all the truth. He will not speak on his own; he will speak only what he hears, and he will tell you what is yet to come" (John 16:13). Notice that Jesus referred to the Holy Spirit as "the Spirit of truth" (also John 14:17; 15:26). Later that same evening, Jesus mentioned God's word of truth (John 17:17). The Spirit of truth and the Word of truth; practically, this means we'll never face a moment in life when God's Word leads us one way and God's Spirit guides us another. The Spirit will never prompt us to do anything that is contrary to God's Word. According to Paul, the Spirit doesn't oppose the Word; he wields the Word (Ephesians 6:17)!

GOD'S PEOPLE

The spiritual life was never meant to be a solitary, independent experience. We were designed for intimate relationships, created for life in interdependent community with God and others. This is why Paul ingeniously likened the people of God to a body—with Christ as the head, and each person as a distinct part (see 1 Corinthians 12). It's a brilliant analogy. You don't have to be enrolled in medical school to know that a severed finger, a plucked-out eyeball, or a surgically removed liver wouldn't survive very long out there in the world, riding around in an Uber or sitting in some coffee shop all by itself! Each body part needs vital connection with all the others to function healthily, properly, and effectively.

> **The Word of God shows us the way to live. The Spirit of God empowers us to live that way. The people of God come along side us as we walk by faith.**

In the same way, we believers desperately need one another. This surely explains why—dozens of times—the New Testament writers emphasize all the things that followers of Jesus are to do for "each other" or for "one another." It's through actions like accepting each other, loving one another, showing hospitality, forgiving, encouraging, serving, teaching, modeling, correcting, and praying for one another that the community of faith helps us grow. We could think about it this way: The Word of God shows us the way to live. The Spirit of God empowers us to live that way. The people of God come along side us as we walk by faith.

We all need God's people speaking truth into our scared, sometimes stubborn hearts. We need others to whisper encouragement into our worn-out souls. We need wiser saints who can share their wisdom. King Solomon understood the importance of counselors, mentors, and elders, writing this nugget of wisdom: "Plans fail for lack of counsel, but with many advisers they succeed" (Proverbs 15:22).

It comes down to this: Do you really want to know and do God's will for your life? Then get in a Bible study with a group of Spirit-led believers. The Word of God, the Spirit of God, and the people of God—that's the trifecta of knowing God's will!

GOD'S MISSION

A thirty-thousand-foot view of the life and ministry of Jesus shows his mission as being one of seeking and saving the lost (Luke 19:10). How'd he go about accomplishing this? He began by calling people to repent, believe the gospel (the good news), and follow him (Mark 1:14–17). After dying on the cross to take away the sins of the world, Jesus rose from the dead. Before returning to heaven he told his disciples (all those who *did* believe in him and followed him) to repeat the process of going and making other disciples all over the earth (Matthew 28:18–20).

That concise overview would seem to give us a broad outline for the life of a Christ follower, or we might say, a believer's job description. We should be devoted to two tracks that are both God's will for our lives:

THE MATURITY TRACK	THE MISSION TRACK
"Come and be my disciple."	"Go and make disciples."
Knowing Jesus and growing in the faith	Helping others know Jesus and grow in the faith
A life with Jesus	A life for Jesus

We can't say it enough: So much of God's will for our lives has already been revealed in God's Word.

- We were created by and for God. Colossians 1:16
- We have been designed to glorify him and to love him with all our hearts. Isaiah 43:7; Mark 12:28–30
- We've been called to follow Jesus and help others do likewise. Matthew 28:18–20
- We've been instructed to love each other and to serve others with all the blessings and resources God has given us. John 13:34–35; 1 Peter 4:11

These things will always be true, no matter where or if you go to college, regardless of whom you marry or don't marry, irrespective of what job you choose or what your zip code is.

> **"Here's how to determine God's will for your life: Go wherever your gifts will be exploited the most."**
>
> **JOHN STOTT**

The mission God has given us as followers of Jesus means that we need to think differently about the decisions we make daily. What if we rephrased the questions we typically ask when wrestling with big choices in life?

- Instead of asking, "Which of these two job possibilities pays better?" ask, "Where can I see myself having the biggest impact for Christ?"
- Instead of asking, "Should I marry this (attractive, fun, interesting) person?" ask, "Can I see the two of us growing spiritually together and serving God effectively together?"
- Instead of asking, "Should I buy that newer, bigger house?" ask, "Would that bigger mortgage payment stretch me financially to the point that I could no longer be as generous as I have been?"

HOW DID GOD REVEAL HIS WILL IN BIBLE TIMES?

MEANS OF REVELATION	DESCRIPTION	EXAMPLES
Theophanies	Theophanies were appearances by God in human form. Some theologians believe these may have been appearances by the pre-incarnate Christ.	Genesis 18:1–3; 32:24–30
Voice	God spoke to people, giving them directives, promises, covenants, and insight into what would happen. Around ninety times from Genesis to Deuteronomy, we find the phrase, "the LORD spoke to Moses."	Exodus 6:28 1 Samuel 3:1–14
Angels	Heavenly messengers (angels) were sent by God to reveal his plans to his people.	Genesis 19:1 Luke 2:10–11
Dreams	God unveiled his plans and purposes in special dreams and through those whom God gifted with interpreting those dreams.	Gen. 41:15–16 Daniel 2:26–28 Matthew 1:19–21

MEANS OF REVELATION	DESCRIPTION	EXAMPLES
Miracles	God employed miracles, also called *signs*. Sometimes his will was confirmed through very unique signs, such as Gideon putting out fleeces for reassurance about what God was calling him to do.	Exodus 4:9 Judges 6:37–40 John 20:30–31
Writing	God gave Israel a comprehensive code of conduct (the Law), even writing part of it on stone tablets. King Belshazzar in the Bible saw a giant, mysterious hand write messages on a plastered wall!	Exodus 31:18 Daniel 5:5
Objects	God authorized the use of the Urim and Thummim, which were tokens or stones that somehow (no one knows for sure how) helped disclose God's will. God also guided his people through the casting of lots, an ancient version of flipping a coin or rolling dice.	Exodus 28:30 Numbers 27:21 Proverbs 16:33 Acts 1:26

MEANS OF REVELATION	DESCRIPTION	EXAMPLES
Prophets	God spoke through prophets and seers, both through their words and through their strange actions—their "sign acts" or object lessons.	2 Kings 3:11 Jeremiah 42:3–4 Isaiah 20:2–4 Ezekiel 4:1–17
Visions	God gave some people supernatural, visual glimpses of things to come and divine commands to obey.	Isaiah 1:1 Ezekiel 8:3 Jeremiah 13:4–7 Acts 9:1–19; 16:9–10

HOW CAN WE DISCERN GOD'S WILL?

Unlike the original followers of Christ, we don't have Jesus physically with us. We can't look into his eyes and hear him speak audibly. On the contrary, we live in a noisy, modern, distracting world that confronts us daily with a multitude of voices and choices.

Thus we need *discernment*.

Discernment is the ability to distinguish and decide between that which is true, wise, and good and that which is false, foolish, and evil. God actually wants all of his children to develop and exercise this ability. Otherwise, why did the apostle Paul pray for the Christians in Philippi: "That your love may abound more and more in knowledge and depth of insight, so that you may be able to discern what is best and may be pure and blameless for the day of Christ" (Philippians 1:9–10)?

We bring up discernment here because this is the skill that will help us move through life making decisions that make God and others—and ourselves—smile. How do we cultivate this holy skill? We saturate our minds with God's Word. We let his truth become the lens through which we view the world. Then, as we move through the world, we yield ourselves to God's Spirit again and again, moment by moment inviting him to prompt us, empower us, and lead us (and to elbow us in the soul when we stray). The more we do this, the better we get at discernment. Also, whenever we find discerning people, we follow them around and watch them like hawks. "Whoever walks with the wise becomes wise" (Proverbs 13:20 ESV).

DISCERNING GOD'S WILL: WHAT TO PAY ATTENTION TO

Godly Advice

We've already mentioned the importance of seeking godly advice, but it bears repeating. After you've prayerfully thought through a course of action, seek input and advice from spiritually wise friends and trusted mentors. Remember that human nature is to gravitate toward those who will tell us what we want to hear. So seek honest, genuine feedback.

In doing this, however, it's important to keep in mind that people aren't *always* right and sometimes they suggest wrong or unwise actions. Let's say, after much prayerful reflection, you start down a path that you really sense is in the will of God. You have some normal trepidation, but overall your choice feels right. Suppose, then, a friend unexpectedly steps forward to express concerns. What does this mean? How should you interpret this event? Should you change your plans? Try this: Fight the urge to become defensive. Ask some clarifying questions. Listen with an open heart and mind. Take some time to prayerfully consider your friend's concerns. After all that, if you decide it's wisest to proceed, be gracious. Express appreciation for your friend's concern. Then gently, humbly, yet firmly, say something like, *I realize I'm not perfect when it comes to following God's guidance, but I am going this direction because right now, this is what I genuinely believe is wisest and best.* Ultimately, your responsibility is to please God, not your friends. In the end, we have to answer to him, not other people.

Now if five of your wisest, most trusted friends are discouraging a chosen course of action, that might be something different altogether. That could be God pulling out all the stops to get your attention!

"For lack of guidance a nation falls, but victory is won through many advisers."
PROVERBS 11:14

THE SPIRITUAL GIFT OF DISCERNMENT

All believers are to cultivate the skill of discernment; however, some Christians possess this ability to a remarkable degree. In Paul's letter to the Corinthian believers, he discusses the topic of spiritual gifts, which are God-given abilities for building up the body of Christ.

> A spiritual gift is given to each of us so we can help each other. To one person the Spirit gives the ability to give wise advice; to another the same Spirit gives a message of special knowledge. The same Spirit gives great faith to another. . . . He gives someone else the ability to discern whether a message is from the Spirit of God or from another spirit. (1 Corinthians 12:7–10 NLT)

God endows some believers with an unusual ability to discern between right and wrong, spiritual truth and spiritual error. When led by the Holy Spirit, they understand when a plan fits with God's will and know when a new teaching contradicts the teachings of the Christian faith. It's as if the indwelling Holy Spirit has given these folks a "bogus theology detector" or a "bad decision buzzer!"

Though even these Christians are, of course, still fallible, it's a good (and biblical) idea to pay extra attention to what they say.

Peace from God

This is a matter of paying close attention to your heart and to which courses of action feel "off" and which ones bring an undeniable sense of peace and rightness. However, keep in mind that doing God's will is sometimes scary and not calming; consider Jesus wrestling with God's will, and even sweating blood in Gethsemane (Luke 22:44)! Pray for a peace from God that transcends any scary situation.

"Do not be anxious about anything, but in every situation, by prayer and petition, with thanksgiving, present your requests to God. And the peace of God, which transcends all understanding, will guard your hearts and your minds in Christ Jesus."

PHILIPPIANS 4:6–7

Spiritual Promptings

Without question, the indwelling Holy Spirit—always in perfect harmony with the truth of God's Word—prompts believers, impresses and burdens us, and puts checks on our spirits. Sometimes we get an overwhelming sense that we need to do (or not do) something. Listen carefully to these holy nudges. But realize that not every internal urge is from God. Any whim or idea or notion needs to be prayerfully and carefully analyzed in light of God's Word.

"And now, compelled by the Spirit, I [Paul] am going to Jerusalem, not knowing what will happen to me there."
ACTS 20:22

Good Sense

This is using our God-given intellect to take into account all the available facts and to be logical and sensible. It's thoughtfully considering all you've learned, your life experiences, and your past mistakes to make informed, God-honoring decisions. This is what the book of Proverbs calls prudence: "The wisdom of the prudent is to give thought to their ways" (Proverbs 14:8).

But even Proverbs warns us not to trust too much in what we think we've got all figured out: "Trust in the LORD with all your heart and lean not on your own understanding" (Proverbs 3:5). Remember that God's ways are much higher than ours (Isaiah 55:9).

"Good sense is a fountain of life to him who has it."
PROVERBS 16:22 ESV

Sovereign Circumstances

This involves carefully reflecting on situations, and prayerfully considering how God might be leading you through those circumstances. Ask God to show you how he is working in your life, to help you see which doors he is opening and which ones he is closing (James 1:5).

Remember, however, that obstacles don't always mean *stop*, and clear roads don't always mean *go*. God sometimes leads his people down paths that seem, at first, like big mistakes or colossal wastes of time. Think, for example, of the

ancient Israelites leaving Egypt and almost immediately finding themselves trapped between the Red Sea and the pursuing Egyptian army. It seemed like a divine disaster, when in truth, it was just the opposite. God did the impossible: "The LORD drove the sea back with a strong east wind and it turned into dry land. The waters were divided and the Israelites went through the sea on dry ground" (Exodus 14:21–22).

We can't immediately declare that something "must not be God's will" based on temporary confusion or difficulty in the moment. Sometimes we can see how God was working in our lives only in hindsight.

> "I am Thy servant to do Thy will, and that will is sweeter to me than position or riches or fame, and I choose it above all things on Earth or in Heaven."
>
> A. W. TOZER

So if you're in a tough spot, try not to panic or turn away. Pray for God's direction and protection. Ask him for enough clarity and courage to take the next right step. Follow the next thing God reveals or the wisest path you can see before you. If you keep trusting and walking, by the end of this life (or at least in the life to come), you will be able to see how God used even the frustrating and painful periods for his glory, and yours and others' good. In all situations that you face, pray as Jesus taught his followers: "Your kingdom come, your will be done" (Matthew 6:10).

"We know that in all things God works
for the good of those who love him,
who have been called
according to his purpose."
ROMANS 8:28

GOD'S WILL: MAKING THE WHOLE TRIP

Author E. L. Doctorow once gave some famous writing advice that is applicable to anyone trying to discover and obey God's will.

Doctorow said, "Writing a novel is like driving a car at night. You can only see as far as your headlights, but you can make the whole trip that way."

What a great word picture! When we think about our lives and our futures, we're reminded that God alone knows what's down the road. None of us knows the twists and turns that lie ahead. But we can see the situations facing us right now, and in each moment we can determine to make a choice that honors God and blesses others. If we keep doing that, moment by moment, day by day, we'll make the whole trip.

> "The will of God will not take us where the grace of God cannot sustain us."
>
> BILLY GRAHAM

Most believers secretly wish that God would give them a clear, detailed itinerary for life. Instead, God gives us a flashlight (a "lamp," his Word; Psalm 119:105) and he offers us an invisible guide (the Holy Spirit; John 16:13). Using these and other resources like the community of believers, we're called make the wisest decisions we can based on what God says and shows us. Pastor and author Francis Chan has pointed out that it's a lot easier to sit around thinking, *I wonder what God wants me doing for the rest of my life?* Instead, we should be asking ourselves, *What do I need to be doing right now and for the next ten minutes?* The point is this: God's will for yesterday is behind you. God's will for tomorrow is not yet your concern. What you have is right now, this moment. Make it your goal to do the next right thing.

We don't have to see far down the road. We just need to see what is before us now. And we need to keep

in mind that God may suddenly take us in a wholly different direction tomorrow. Be okay with that. See that as part of the great adventure of walking "by faith, not by sight" (2 Corinthians 5:7).

"May the God of peace . . . equip you with everything good for doing his will, and may he work in us what is pleasing to him, through Jesus Christ, to whom be glory for ever and ever. Amen."

HEBREWS 13:20–21

10 QUESTIONS TO ASK YOURSELF WHEN GOD'S WILL ISN'T CLEAR

The Bible is explicit about many things, but some life situations are more gray than black and white because they're not discussed or "covered" specifically in Scripture. When facing decisions where God's Word isn't specific and overt, these ten questions can be great diagnostic tools.

1. **How can I bring God the most glory here?**

   Sometimes one particular option is more honoring to God than the others because, for example, it requires more trust or stepping away from temptation.

   "Do it all for the glory of God."
   1 CORINTHIANS 10:31

2. **Am I just relying on my own understanding or am I trusting in the Lord?**

   Often we have to act without having every fact or piece of data. We have to trust God.

   "Trust in the Lord with all your heart and lean not on your own understanding."
   PROVERBS 3:5

3. **Am I primarily trying to please God or please people?**

Our ultimate audience is the Lord, not our friends, parents, mentors, classmates, or neighbors.

"We make it our goal to please him . . . for we all must appear before the judgment seat of Christ."
2 CORINTHIANS 5:9–10

4. **Is this a case of "seems too good to be true"?**

We have to remember that our world is alluring and under the control of a destructive deceiver whose goal is to ruin our lives.

"There is a way that appears right, but in the end it leads to death."
PROVERBS 14:12

5. **Does this choice move me toward or away from a holier life?**

   We are called to become more and more like Jesus in our thoughts, words, and deeds. Some choices facilitate that better than others.

"Be holy in all you do."
1 PETER 1:15

6. **Will this decision damage the reputation of Christ—or my own, as one of his followers?**

   We are to be above reproach in all we do.

"Among you there must not be even a hint of sexual immorality, or of any kind of impurity, or of greed, because these things are improper for God's holy people."
EPHESIANS 5:3

7. Might this course of action start me down a path that would be dangerous to my soul?

It's important to be aware of the weaknesses of our flesh and the temptations that often trip us up.

"Do not set foot on the path of the wicked."
PROVERBS 4:14

8. Would this choice cause a "weaker" believer to "stumble," to violate his or her conscience and emulate my behavior?

Love requires that I sometimes voluntarily limit my freedom for the sake of others.

"Be careful, however, that the exercise of your rights does not become a stumbling block to the weak."
1 CORINTHIANS 8:9

9. Even if this decision isn't sinful per se, is it a wise course of action?

Some choices are clearly wrong; but even among the options that are acceptable, some are better or best. Followers of Jesus should pursue the way of wisdom (Proverbs 16:16).

"'I have the right to do anything,' you say—but not everything is beneficial . . . not everything is constructive."
1 CORINTHIANS 10:23

10. Would more mature believers endorse or encourage this?

Since we are surrounded by older and wiser saints, it's foolish not to seek out their sage counsel.

"Listen to advice and accept discipline."
PROVERBS 19:20

20 QUESTIONS FOR FURTHER REFLECTION AND DISCUSSION

1. On a scale of one to ten, with one being "I'm the rookiest of rookies" and ten being "I'm an old, experienced pro," how would you rate yourself when it comes to discerning God's will in decision-making?

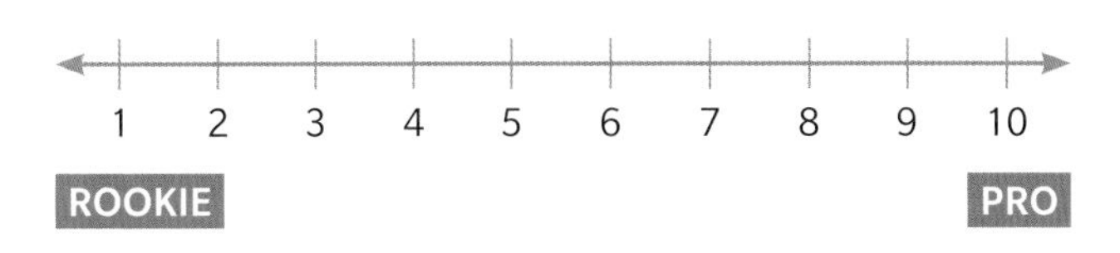

2. What specific, confusing decisions are you facing in your life right now?

3. What factors typically make it difficult for you to know the best course of action?

4. What spiritual practices or resources do you find most helpful in discerning God's will?

5. What role does the Holy Spirit play in helping us understand God's truth and find God's will?

6. Why can we be sure that God's Spirit and God's Word will never lead us in two different directions at the same time?

7. What helps you continue to follow God's will during times when his will leads to or involves suffering?

8. Suppose instead of giving us his Word and his Spirit, God supplied each of his children with a personalized app that dinged and buzzed with precise messages moment by moment, telling us exactly what to think, do, and say in every situation. What do you imagine would happen to our faith and to our relationship with God?

9. What advice would you give a person who wants to serve God in some capacity and volunteer their time and resources, but doesn't have a clear sense of where or how God wants them to serve?

10. Do you think God has a "soul mate" for each person? Should we be looking and/or waiting for "Mr./Ms. Right"?

11. Do you think if a believer truly loves God and has a "not my will but your will be done" mind-set, he or she will end up in the right place even if there are mistakes and wrong turns along the way? Why or why not?

12. Someone once speculated, "If we're currently disregarding the things God has clearly revealed for us to do in his Word, why should he reveal any more of his will for our lives?" What do you think about that idea?

13. Read Philippians 1:6. This Bible verse gives us a glimpse of God's will or plan for each believer. How specifically and practically today can you cooperate with (rather than fight against) God's desire to complete the good work he's begun in you?

14. Read 1 John 5:14–15. How can we know when we're praying "according to God's will"? Can you give some examples?

15. Read James 1:5–7. Why is doubt or unbelief so detrimental to seeking God's direction?

16. Do you know any Christians who have that extra-special, God-given ability to discern—to correctly understand situations, plans, and messages and say, "that's a bad idea" or "that's the way to go"?

17. What wrong thoughts, actions, or habits in your life fight against your ability to discern the will of God? What can you do to change them?

18. What's your best story of God showing you his will for you?

19. Based on what you know of God's Word, what are some things that you know for sure are the will of God for your life today?

20. What tools and resources discussed in this book do you think will prove most helpful in your current search to know God's will?

Image Credits

Images used under license from Shutterstock.com: Pajor Pawel, page header image; Mimadeo, cover, pages 3, 5, 6, 8, 27, 33, 36, 39; gopixa, 7 (top); Amanda Carden, 7 (bottom), 17 (bottom); Tapui, 9; Ape Man, back cover, 10, 14; cherezoff, 11; frankie's, 12; Julia Shepeleva, 17 (top); Benevolente82, 19; mapman, 21; Dmitry Pistrov, 24; Billion Photos, 29, 65 (top); Sashkin, 34; Mega Pixel, 46; Pakhnyushchy, 49; Drakuliren, 54; Rachata Sinthopachakul, 56; palidachan, 58; Dream Perfection, 61; Helder Almeida, 65 (bottom); Love You Stock, 69; Melinda Nagy, 71; Brent Wong, 75; Deer worawut, 76; nikolay100, 79; StepanPopov, 85.

MADE EASY

by Rose Publishing

BIBLE STUDY MADE EASY
A step-by-step guide to studying God's Word
ISBN 9781628623437

THE BOOKS OF THE BIBLE MADE EASY
Quick summaries of all 66 books of the Bible
ISBN 9781628623420

HOW WE GOT THE BIBLE MADE EASY
Key events in the history of the Bible
ISBN 9781628628241

KNOWING GOD'S WILL MADE EASY
Answers to tough questions about God's will
ISBN 9781628628234

UNDERSTANDING THE HOLY SPIRIT MADE EASY
Who the Holy Spirit is and what he does
ISBN 9781628623444

WORLD RELIGIONS MADE EASY
30 religions and how they compare to Christianity
ISBN 9781628623451

www.hendricksonrose.com